The Gizmos' Trip

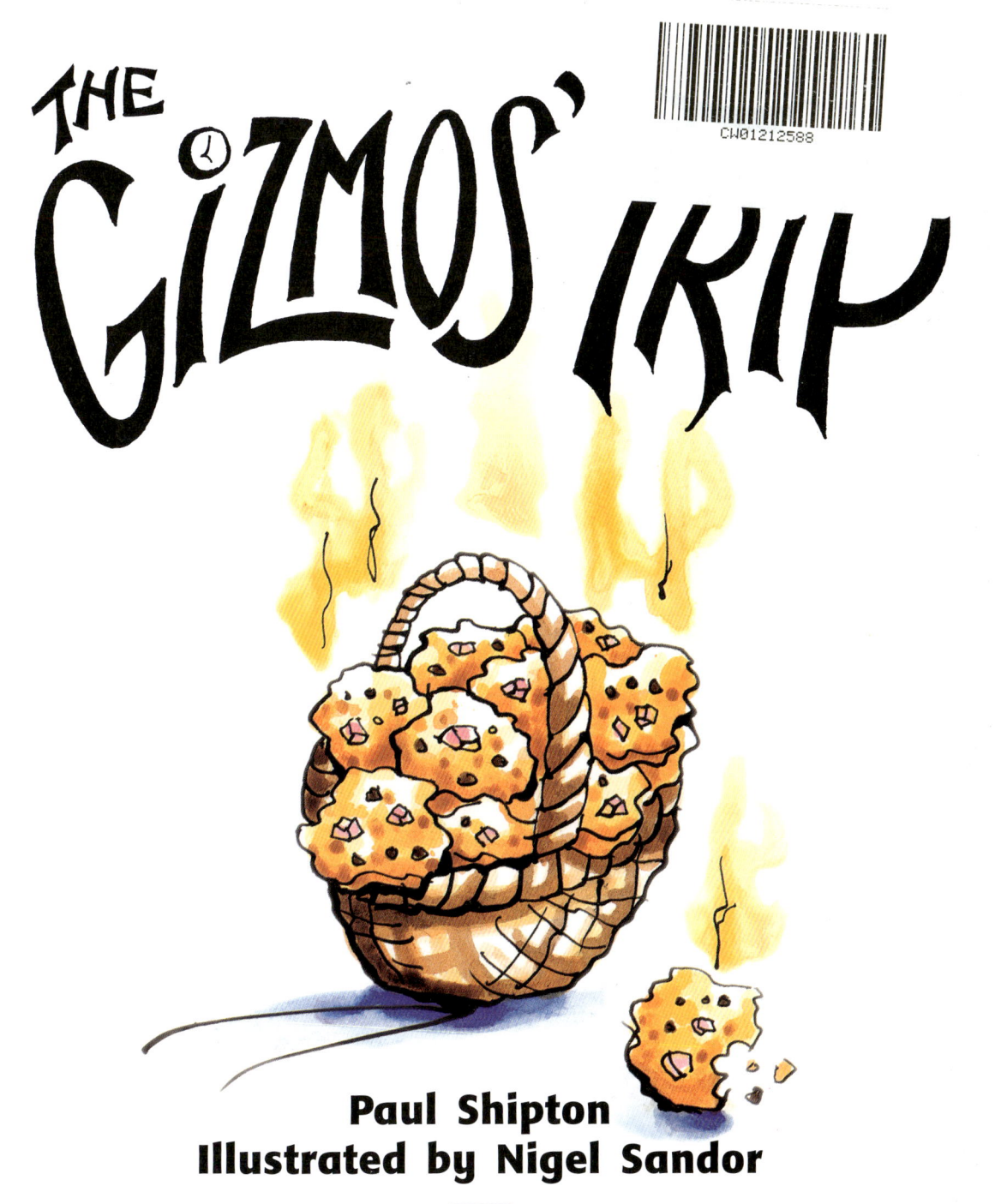

Paul Shipton
Illustrated by Nigel Sandor

R RIGBY

Chapter 1

One day, I was reading a comic book on my bed. Suddenly there was a flash of light and my mum was in my room.

"Where's your homework, Albert Gizmo?" she asked.

I was too surprised to answer. "Er . . . how did you get in here?" I asked.

Mum grinned. "This is my latest invention. It's a teleporter!"

"That's nice," I said. "What does it do?"

"It can take us anywhere in the world, instantly," replied Mum.

I sighed. Life isn't always easy when your mother is an inventor.

"I want us to try it out," Mum said. "Where's your dad?"

"In the kitchen," I said.

Mum stopped smiling. "He . . . he isn't cooking, is he?" she asked.

"I hope not," I said.

Our dad is good at lots of things, but cooking isn't one of them.

After Mum left, my sister Marie came in, carrying a basket.

"What's THAT?" she asked pointing at the machine.

"Mum's latest invention."

Marie wasn't surprised. We were used to Mum's inventions.

She held out a basket. "Have a biscuit," she said.

I took one and I ALMOST bit into it. Then I saw the smile on Marie's face.

"Hold on," I said. "Who baked these?"

Marie grinned. "Dad!"

"Yuck!" I dropped the biscuit and jumped back in horror. Unfortunately, I bumped the control panel on Mum's machine. "Oops!" I said.

There was no time to fix it. The next moment, Mum and Dad came into my room. Dad was carrying another basket.

"Did you try a biscuit?" Dad asked.

"Yes," I lied. "Very good. What's in them?"

"Chocolate chips and tuna," he said.

I felt sick.

"Come on, everyone into the machine," said Mum. She started pressing buttons. At least everything seemed to work OK.

"Let's go somewhere nice," she said. She pushed one more button.

Chapter 2

There was a terrible crackle, and my room disappeared in a flash of light.

When I opened my eyes, we were out in the country.

"What a lovely spot!" said Dad.

Dad spread a picnic blanket near the top of a hill. "Let's eat. I've made a lovely picnic," said Dad.

"Um . . . we're not hungry, thanks," I said. I sat and looked at the view.

"What's that?" asked Marie, pointing at a dot in the sky.

"A pigeon?" I said. The dot grew bigger.

"A duck?" said Dad.

"An eagle?" said Marie.

It flew closer. It wasn't a bird at all!

"A pterodactyl!" shouted Mum. "We're in the past!"

"The past? Oops!" I said again.

The reptile flew by.

"I don't understand," said Mum. "We were supposed to travel in space, not time. The machine went wrong. But how?"

There wasn't time to answer, because an ear-splitting roar came from the forest.

"I think now is a good time to leave," said Dad.

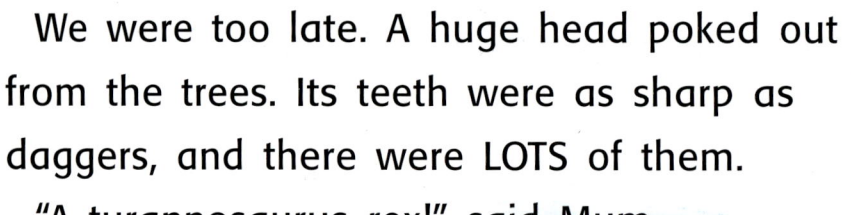

We were too late. A huge head poked out from the trees. Its teeth were as sharp as daggers, and there were LOTS of them.

"A tyrannosaurus rex!" said Mum.

We were too busy running to listen.

The tyrannosaurus might not have tasted humans before, but it wanted to taste us! It ran quickly on its giant legs. We would never reach Mum's machine in time!

We had come here for a picnic. Now we were going to BE the picnic!

Suddenly the dinosaur stopped. It bent its head down to our picnic blanket and sniffed deeply. What was it doing?

Suddenly I understood. I grabbed the basket from Dad's arm. Then I threw the biscuits onto the ground.

"Run!" I shouted. We all ran towards Mum's machine.

When we got to the machine, the tyrannosaurus had reached the biscuits. It was eating them as if they were the most delicious food it had ever tasted.

Mum pushed the control buttons quickly.

"Quick!" cried Marie. "I think it's looking for pudding!"

It was true. The dinosaur was moving towards us again. It still looked hungry. It had almost reached us when Mum pressed the last button.

We heard the dinosaur's roar of anger and the crackle of electricity. Then we were safely back in our own house.

The next day we went to the museum. It was Dad's idea.

"Why is your dad so interested in dinosaurs now?" asked Mum.

Marie and I laughed. "They're the only things that ever liked his biscuits!"